GROWING

Dide

ISBN: 978-1-915079-27-5

Cover design by Aaron Kent

Edited & Typeset by Aaron Kent

Broken Sleep Books (2022)

Broken Sleep Books Ltd
Rhydwen,
Talgarreg,
SA44 4HB
Wales

Contents

For space – cosmic, natural, personal: to be able to be oneself

Growing

Dide

Symbol, noun, representative
- *= a thing that represents or stands for something else (Google Online Dictionary)*
- *= something that is used to represent a quality or an idea (Cambridge Dictionary)*

A representation, mark, transmission, gesture, sound is not a thought

All communication is representational transmission

Counting the silence ///

like music // like the rests in between music / like the timed semibreve
of silence ////
/
/
Skip a few staves // empty lines like railroad tracks waiting to see where
to lead //
/
A dotted minim ///
/
Where's the line from noise? /
/
If experiential silence is just another kind of noise /
/
If something of a whole is always created in the mind ///
/

 = "

Armchairs for lonely people

have sides that cardboard box, making you feel like keys that have fallen in too deep, into the plush of velvet meat that has presence to hide behind or, in this case, take the pressure off to be human, instead the eye of a peephole, *umarmt*.

If only we could always wear a velour armchair around us.

Ɔ = A

GREEN CUT MOAT

Round once, and then again, you go,
circling the house like a red pen, marking
out job ads in newspapers. He follows,
our growing friend-child, the veil bearer.
His hair shortens as his height lengthens
and new clothes appear with each loop
of the year. This is you playing grown up.
This is me, laughing, doing the same.
We're becoming real, we are real people,
with cars and houses and lawnmowers that
bandage me in. Inside the house, I sit, my
bruises wrapped like a Christmas present,
smiling every time you hula-hoop with the
noisy grass-eater. Our green cut moat is our
wedding ring, haloing commitment to our
lives, together, like gold leaf to a Bible

= L

Fruit salad massacre

My thumb penetrates bruised blood red
as juice splutters and pops

on the cold granite worktop
innards souring to vulva-purple

only flesh remains –

                The knife
                        between, like a lighthouse

signals port-coloured confluence
of those destroyed, animal and mineral,

floating to the left, nearer the body's heart

if life can be sliced from biology

kiss-me-fuchsia swells each hemisphere
of the <3-shaped cherry in my palm.

ࠁ = L

=

These lines like two adjacent tightropes, brand their equals into skin, failing to match perfectly, as the hand must've wobbled, with a view so great, since an abyss can always terrify. The knives had gleamed their devilish smile, to trap soul-kites in the underworld. The consequence, a prideful addition, while the subtraction of self-worth swelled up and down, like the frequency monitors in hospitals, where life – and psyche – teeter.

$-\rho$ = C

WOODLAND

What struck, was the lack of trees, not even felled for tables,
geometric lines from a Mondrian bore down in grey, white and off-white.

I've come to see a friend, I said.
After a day's work and an evening's swim, the unit was still *rayonn*ing
light like a child's crayon drawing of the Sun;

the only giveaway of the darkness inside was the emptiness of the corridors.
A fat man, whose belly craved freedom as much as burgers and didn't
like being squished under the CCTV desk,

went through the protocol, and I felt the rush of excitement I imagined
some felt visiting prison. It was no different really.

Locked in a dog's cage in the back of a black van during pick-up. Violently
restrained. Liberties stripped. Your life putty in their gloved hands.
Excitement turned to disgust and anger.

I thought back to the Victorian asylums whose eugenics had won.
I thought forward to my friend, whose mind they tried to get to by
controlling her weight. After an hour,

with my friend fretting over if I'd had enough tea, and chatting with a
few other patients, whose heaviness bungeed their faces long, time was up,
visiting hour over.

As I drove off, a strange symbol lit up, one I'd never seen before, and
the car stopped. The thought of skipping it never entered my mind.
And true to form, the flash disappeared.

$\lfloor \bullet \rfloor$ = O

THE CLINIC, HER

surgeon hair badger-tailed and crinkled
from the spaced-slumber the night before
I remember white
were the walls
and other instruments
of medicine
silver, too
young and cool
she was at Kurfürstenstraße after all
it shouldn't have surprised me
this was where hookers gave blowjobs in broad daylight
I think I might have seen one or two
I don't remember that
as well as the white
and silver
the cold colours hugged me
and her breezy voice
the place had the coolness of a spring clean

it's been five years
since I left
the streets of fears behind Arab men who spat
and other polaroid images
that fade in and out

the covered canal where pain tunnelled and came out
the other end, to tunnel again

happen once, and it'll stick
with the sweetness that lures wasps
happen more, privilege nicked

♀ = M

I return, to the silver chrome handles
the white disposable paper
on which you lie and open
and feel like a throne
play sleeping lions to cope and –

an orange with missing segments screening
how I can't, or thereupon moan

the thrift store after the ordeal

the bulbous lights of the street theatre

flash unknowing unknown passers-by
such as the greasy pulled-back pony
of the blonde-haired phony with cigarette
-stained teeth
and shoulders hunched
vest too

a place I visited
only a handful of times
where the holy fruit was washed and cleaned and investigated
during the eternity
that was white
and is white
and will always be white
the still time before the party begins.

ϕ = M

ALL THE MEN EVER

(i)   a type of human like a mallard
that's not all brown
car-dealer, scrum-prop, a chiral molecule,
which might mean something to chemists
or 'Breaking Bad' viewers,
or crystal meth users, sometimes called
enantiomers, which reminds me of anteaters
can be anteaters too, this time
all shades of brown

(i)   lasting forever
(ii)   unable to be killed like a man
like the Morse Code of staggered consciousness
– a temporary finite imagining the infinite –

like those welcome collages at airport arrivals
of faces made up of many
he has a piece of all
and adds further still

can be personal – past partners catching the light in the
glint of a companion mosaic – or societal

inclusive of Harriet with her penis playing the trombone
and Lake taking tablets to grow theirs
like tomatoes on dark vines
after pink meant candy-wife
and blue, Ken
stuck in vows
with bubble gum

$$\multimap\quad = U$$

(An imagined) meeting

… yeah, come for dinner one day,
you and her will sit on the garden chairs
ceilidhing round the table
we've been meaning to oil, and
will knit stories around the fire
of Mediterranean platters.
The grass will begin a clandestine affair
with toes of the greenest kind
while music loud edges on its leash
from howls of the kitchen grind
and the daffs trenching us in
cup their ears to listen.

… no, you don't need to worry
it won't be strange or like old times,
you'll lean to her and I'll to him
like plants to the Sun
and I'll show you what we've made here
and you'll close your eyes and hum
of all the things that are not
and could not, it turns, have been,
you'll like the view, the walk too
on the water's other side,
then you'll remember and push
plate morsels with your knife,
leftovers of another lot.
I'll hand your coats and off you'll go
though goodbyes were long ago,
you'll see yourself in him, a man
so different, so planted to the place,
that you'll wonder, if the soil grew him,
like potatoes you dig with toil.

♉ = N

A HUNDRED BOLSHEVIKS

, and like a vaccine, it ink-jots its poison like the squid, a *poisson*, it is,
for me.
It is, for others too,
a *poisson* we cannot catch, so slippery it slides snot-loose
while we crave for a bite.
Did it used to be like this? you ask – but no, preterm plucks
the miscarriage of grain.
It rises, up the throat, rises with the backwash of desire, of wanting
to fit, of tasting the greenness of the other grass.
But this wheat is too green, it revolts in me with the fervour of a hundred
Bolsheviks.
It kicks with the parasite too early, lobbying, too eager, transforming,
how what we thought was gold of old has milled,
and like a vaccine repelled, juts out cold.

$\ulcorner$ = I

She was born on a commune
where the assassination of her father
hung like a flaccid dick
he died 13 years later, unrelated
though conspiracies stuck
like grease to wallpaper
She was bullied / ten years of a stalker – a police file against him /
attempted rape / £30,000 stolen and that wasn't even the time
her flatmate took
her identity, and money too /
She's been homeless though never thought it /
She has BPD, PMDD, mild Asperger's and what else not /
Physical too, in the past, she couldn't walk or bend her back
MRIs, X-rays, of a body noted athletic /
She's travelled the world, studied at the best – precocious little shit /
She came back, became a wife, to the whole county of Suffolk
No fucking, just ignoring
like all her youth's prizes meant ash /
She has a strange relationship with her mother
who had a strange relationship with her father
who turned to piss and flushed down the drain
but I never mention any of this

$$-\rho \ = C$$

In the commune

The language of politics was my lullaby , my Sufi ascent from the baobab tree to ancestral spirits robbing thoughts, like magpies, eggs, from the living until they too die and rob , my heritage, not of tin roofs and stampeding hooves of poverty of fishing rag-tailed and speaking crêpe creole of de sweet chilli burst of Auntie Mattie's cooking dat scorches memory in blander times in clouded drizzly mid-October bleach , my tales I did not know well enough to entertain or teach with a shimmy and a belly wiggle a breast pop and a jingle of the coins lining my buttocks. The domed twirls of the *ezan* chiming five times a day we abhorred, pillows made of Lenin. My baby-speak was of politics, of marching 8 billion by 8 billion hurrah hurrah! , my fleeting aspiration for animals two by two, mother by father, selfish when here I had multiple honorary guardians, aunts and uncles, and brothers and sisters, where here only the cherry tree paired off fruit to be dangled in duo, from ears that looped the hearsay and buried it deep in the gut. Romantic idealism rocked me to and fro. Nightmares, of innocents imprisoned, their families left to the metronomic bars of the onward tide of dissenters disappeared of rats the size of children of crafts – stitched, weaved and braided – of unwanted rubbish turned into want, for instance, wallets with change locked like their makers for instance, pastel paintings scraped like shit stains. I had not the alluring hot coolness, or did not know enough of it, or cared not to market it, no, I had the ga-gas and the goo-goos of politics unsteady on its feet and of grubby fingers drawing all to the whoops and whooshes of fairground descents.

Ӽ = A

Upstage, downstage, and to the right and left

Henrietta Swan Leavitt
Sari Nusseibeh
Lise Meitner
Ibn Khaldun
Nikola Tesla
Oswaldo Guayasamín
Jagadish Chandra Bose
Esther Lederberg
Anne Brontë
Wang Zhenyi
Don Shirley
Saddest of all, those
whose names
smoke off
like the whiff of a
cigar in a mens-only
drawing room.

L = T

[Narrator, prologue:]

In Farsi,

my name means the *power of eyes*,
seer of the future in Sanskrit, and in Turkish,
powerful meaningful beautiful eyes;

my eyes disabled,

hardly see past my nose.

⌐ = I

[Manifesto, body:]

Governance and persistence,

are the two areas,
under which all else falls
like rain beneath the Karman Line

governance of inequalities – gender, race, wealth, neurodiversity

persistence of species, habitat

My name amounts to soothsayer
and I see the ascending linear loops
of the calligrapher: an expansion
of governance and persistence,
with its due dips, like stock
market dives in overall rise,
before, a re-formation of matter.

⌊•⌋ = O

THE DEATH OF LYNN'S ICE CUBE

Exempt, made her feel masculine / Lynn,
bowing down to the pooling carcass / Christmas
gone and Christmas come, how much death / Beth
-leham gave rise to? / Few
fems melted into the liquid unwrapping / mapping
out a crushed murder / further.
Stiletto-stepped, the chance cube cracks / packs
a punch, on the raucous festivity / nativity,
gather up quick to be reborn / Forlorn
tepid water drooling / cooling
the flames of ambition / attrition
crucifies with time / divine.
Domestic trampling at the prescribed hour / flower
from seed, the coming-of-age / beige.
Far-flung, the multi-coloured dreams / weaves
waterway of expectation / elation,
further, further still / till,
goals persist in the mind / prime
dissolves / resolves,
the starlet child / mild-
ly merges into / anew,
a slavish woman / anon
anon.

℧ = N

DEAR ENSŌ,

and as circular as the ensō, you bring us round
        to remembrance,
and as comforting as dimples we've grown up with, we
        join again,
and never mind the distance, between you
        and me,
and even if we look up and see,
        a different slant, tinge or nearness,
and amidst all the change, rest, do we
        regolith admirers,
and no longer calling the other to say
        'Look!'
and no longer thinking of the other, to feel
        connected,
and no, there's no need for all that, for what separates you
        and me?
and just a name and a history and a character
        and…
and just all that, that you might feel is a lot, but
        look again!
and you'll see the dot, the full stop
        of our world of words.
And from that, the gateway to another, with its full stop,
        and that, its own…
and so, the pens of the universe have spiraled, linking,
        cosmic clauses,
and some might think this cause for grief,
        alone in our insignificance,
and yet each alone, do we unite
        under the gaze of fright,
and of hope, of love and of privacy, of health
        and mystery,
and come now, full circle, for you are you and you,
        for you are all possibility,
the moon and the girl who phoned on full moons,
        the seer and the seen,
the rememberer and the remembering, to where, then
        dissolves the **memory?**

$$\Gamma = I$$

...and then evolved man, who lent their name, to hu- and wo-, dominating from the belly of brute, from tools and fire and agriculture and language and pen and then their intellect was kneaded until the knuckled dough of more rose higher, and man tried to turn itself to insan and grew and grew and dropped and grew and grew ... and then evolved man

when will man turn into insan?

✝ = S

Dirac's equation

Lesser known than the cat, the lynx is perhaps greater, as it binds the tiny with the fast, living hidden in the brambles, of those in the know, their diminishing presence, reflecting their diminishing absence.

$$+ \quad = S$$

THE COSMOLOGICAL PRINCIPLE

– assuming the universe is the same everywhere, and in all directions – is like assuming all caves are the same everywhere, and in all directions, from the hexagonal basalt of Fingal's Cave to the sabres of Crystal Cave; or that every city is gridded like New York.

$= Y$

EXPANDING

The universe is growing, so Hubble found in 1929, at a rate slower than a teenage boy, but faster than the halt of adulthood, that no basketball game can undo. It's not expanding, like an accordion, although it might shrink back again, or just

continue, until our minds, burst, from humble

recognition, like Demodex mites, that eat too

much, and explode, into the

big bang of rosacea,

realising, that we really,

don't see

enough.

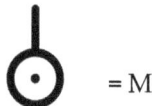 = M

WARNING IF HUMANS BECOME INTERGALACTIC

Earth as a storage file,
a USB stick in space
with all human history
bottled under the
ozone cork, hard to
find the file from the
44th second of the 23rd
minute of the 9th hour
of the 52nd day of the
5th year of the 4th decade
of the 21st century of the
3rd millennium of the ad
infinitum except not ad
infinitum because it's all
there in that filing cabinet
that the humans left when
moving homes, that
poor celestial garage.

γ = B

A child's bedtime story

There was a little boy called Scar. Scar was tough, except for a secret weakness. No one knew, and swarmed around him, like strawberry bushes do, to pick at whim. At night, he was different. It wasn't looney *luna* moon who scared him. Looney *luna* held no sway, how she did over the tides, or sensitive souls half here and half there. Water ebbed in and out, drawn to looney *luna*, like gerbils to peanut butter, while Scar stayed in bed, affixed. Scar was scared of something else. The marks of his fear were found in his eyes, his skin free of his namesake. His eyes twinkled like red traffic lights. His mum told him there were only two, one in his left and one in his right eye, and only they mattered. But he knew there were more; there were many more. When his blackout curtains were lifted and all asleep under their duvets drew hillscapes with their snoring breaths, he was the only one who saw, the glittering clusters, terrifying in their trypophobic magnitude. He tried to bandage his eyes from seeing the tiny billion pinpricks; they dirtied the purity of the night sky. But they followed him, with the power of a disease. One day he realised, it weighed him down more to avoid them than to accept them, and as he went to twitch the curtain, he thought 'could they be my nighttime strawberries?'

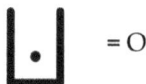

$\lfloor \bullet \rfloor$ = O

THE BEAUTY OF THE UNIVERSE

Choosing principles on beauty is like choosing ice cream on colour.

If imagination is infinite in possibility, as infinite as the number Pi,

and the whole universe, an imagining Solaris...

Beauty brushes understanding into place, taming incomprehensible flyaways.

If a finite boundary is growing infinitely, like weight that scales on...

Occam's Razor, the preference for the simpler with fewer assumptions, is beautiful.

If a universe is always in another, like an Escher painting twisting in on itself,

so that there is never a problem of the outside – the foreigner, what's beyond God,

where God is just the birth of all...

Scientists think Occam's beauty soars because it's testable.

If space and time disappear at the no-boundary, or beyond the boundary,

like visuals in a black vacuum...

Being testable might not always prove truth. The Earth's flatness was testable.

If a twistverse is no more provable than another, a sentiment expressed in many ways...

Is love testable? Most science requires just as many leaps of faith.

If a life form within the verse is no more provable than another,

and if all life forms have some form of consciousness...

 = L

35

JOHN

Did I kill you?

It's amazing how empty I felt, returning home empty-handed;
even more, the strength short-lived motherhood gave,

with you on my breast
than any knife in my fist.

Why did you suddenly think 'enough was enough',
jump straight out, and die?

It happened so quick, I couldn't comprehend, and sat
beside you awhile, as cars drove past the country road.

You'd looked so happy in my arms, blinking every time I checked,
sometimes you shut your eyes.

I had all these dreams: we'd call you 'John',
since we called your brethren P. John.

You'd be the glory of the proletariat,
raising your ancestors to the heights of eagles;

the poster child of symbiosis,
between different kinds of genera.

Did I kill you, little pigeon? Should I have left you by the side
of the road? Did your heart give up, in fright of me?

I saw five splutters of your neck, then nothing more,
only stiffness, and later, an ant beneath you.

⌐ = I

COMRADE

she clasps her child to her bosom
in war-torn jungle conflict zones
scratching that inconsiderate brat of an itch
that whines for attention
as she suckles it quiet,
a bullet fast whizzes past: a rape
of her land, a pillaging of her spoils,
a heated murder;
she clings to the neck of her own mother tree
how her vanquished child before, with her,
her hair falls one by one
like the fire splinters floating down
resting in the burnt soil
of her salacious betrayers,
who see only a gorilla, alone,
in a tall leafless evergreen.

-p = C

0 1 1 2 3 5 8

Male mosquitos are said to hum at D natural, while females at G, two of the most common notes in human song, a fifth, part of the triad, as everyday as arm-stretching when waking up yawning, a musical Fibonacci linking us to mosquitos, dolphins and the growth of mushrooms, like the sequential spiral, the snail, shell and the petals of flowers.

EVERY SCHOOL YEAR MY MUM
REFILLED MY PENCIL CASE

Change is the only constant, the stationary
— horizon —
to the sailed living, of ever-changing particles

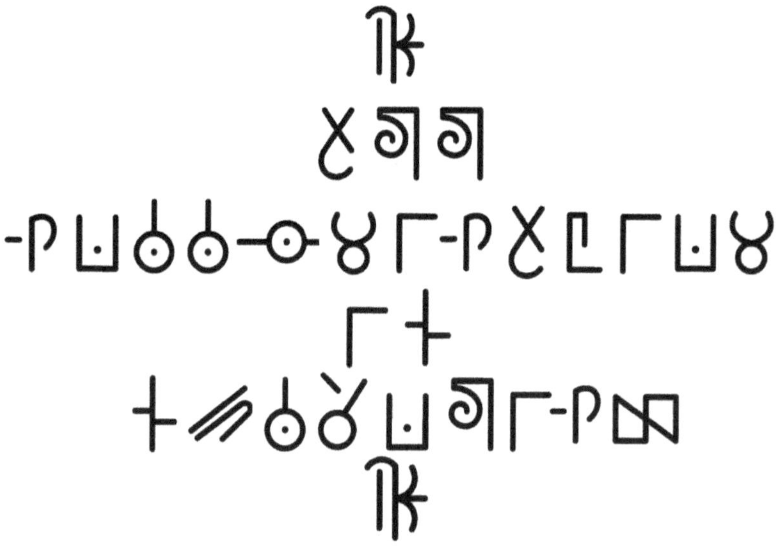

NOTES AND ACKNOWLEDGEMENTS

Notes on poems in order of appearance: Counting the silence / / / – for me, the slash equals a clap; Armchairs for lonely people – *'umarmt'* means 'hugged/put arm around' in German; Woodland – *'rayonn'* comes from the French *'rayonner'* meaning 'to shine', and I like the nod to the Sun's rays; The clinic, her – Kurfürstenstraße is a German street name in the red light district of Berlin; A hundred Bolsheviks – is about rising gluten intolerance in the face of changing quickening wheat production, and *'poisson'* is the French for 'fish'; The first unnamed poem in this pamphlet ('Dirty Washing') – makes personal reference to an ongoing stalker since 2012; The death of Lynn's ice cube – is in honour of all the girls who had to give up their dreams when they turned into women of the home, 'fems' is a shortening of 'feminists', 'female' and 'femme', which is a French word that in English refers to a lesbian whose appearance and behaviour are seen as traditionally feminine; Ensō – 'ensō' is the Japanese for 'circle' and one of the most important symbols in Zen Buddhism, this poem is addressed to the Moon and to a friend who used to phone on full moons, regolith = lunar soil; History lesson – *'insan'* is the ungendered Turkish word for 'man'; Dirac's equation – Dirac's equation, similar to Schrodinger's, was a fundamental victory of theoretical physics, alongside Newton, Maxwell and Einstein's equations, proving the existence of anti-matter and linking the tiny particles of quantum physics with the fast particles of relativity; A child's bedtime story – *'luna'* is the Spanish for 'moon'; the symbolic poem at the end of the pamphlet ('Naming') translates as "All communication is symbolic.".

Acknowledgements in alphabetical order: Rishi Dastidar, Faber Academy, Gryphen Ford for the digitalisation of my invented micro-language, Jen Hadfield and the Arvon Foundation, Wayne Holloway-Smith and our 2021 Monday evening Poetry School group, Ilya Kaminsky for inspiring me to write the last poem ('Naming') in this pamphlet by including sign language symbols in his book *Deaf Republic*, Aaron Kent and Broken Sleep Books for taking a chance on me, Popshot Quarterly magazine for publishing a version of my first unnamed poem in this pamphlet ('Dirty Washing'), the Seamus Heaney Centre and those on the 2020 summer week, in particular Nick Laird, Charles Lang and Stephen Sexton, and Tentacular Magazine for publishing a version of '='.

Special thanks to my mother, father and partner. Thanks also to my family, friends and everybody and everything I've come in contact with in my life.

www.ingramcontent.com/pod-product-compliance
Lightning Source LLC
Chambersburg PA
CBHW040122070426
42448CB00043B/3482